WORLD'S GREATEST ATHLETES

LeBron JAMES

By John Walters

The Child's World
www.childsworld.com

Published in the United States of America by The Child's World®
P.O. Box 326 • Chanhassen, MN 55317-0326
800-599-READ • www.childsworld.com

ACKNOWLEDGMENTS

The Child's World®: Mary Berendes, Publishing Director

Produced by Shoreline Publishing Group LLC
President / Editorial Director: James Buckley, Jr.
Designer: Tom Carling, carlingdesign.com
Cover Art: Slimfilms
Copy Editor: Beth Adelman

Photo Credits:
Cover: AP/Wide World
Interior: Corbis, 23; all other photos by AP/Wide World.

LIBRARY OF CONGRESS
CATALOGING-IN-PUBLICATION DATA

Walters, John (John Andrew)
  LeBron James / by John Walters.
      p. cm. — (The world's greatest athletes)
  Includes bibliographical references and index.
  ISBN 1-59296-756-6 (library bound : alk. paper)
  1. James, LeBron—Juvenile literature. 2. Basketball players—
United States—Biography—Juvenile literature. 3. African American
basketball players—Biography—Juvenile literature. I. Title. II. Series.
  GV884.J36W35 2006
  796.323092—dc22

                                          2006006289

CONTENTS

LeBron James Uncovered

LEBRON JAMES FIRST MADE THE COVER OF SPORTS *Illustrated* magazine in 2002. He was only 17 years old and a high school junior. By then, the Akron, Ohio, native had played in basketball scrimmages against Michael Jordan. He had also attended a Jay-Z concert and hung out with the famous rapper before the show. In 2001, he became the first sophomore to win Ohio's "Mr. Basketball" award, given each year to the state's top high school player.

No wonder that *Sports Illustrated* declared LeBron "The Chosen One."

"At this age LeBron is better than anybody I've seen in 37 years in this sport," Sonny Vaccaro, a high school hoops talent scout, told S.I. "That's including Kevin Garnett and Kobe Bryant and Tracy McGrady."

In the five years since that magazine cover appeared, LeBron has justified the **hype**. He led his high school team, St. Vincent–St. Mary's (SVSM), to two more Ohio state championships. He also was Mr. Basketball two more times.

After high school, he skipped college and went right to the pros, where he's done everything right. After being the first pick in the 2003 NBA draft by the Cleveland Cavaliers, he was the NBA Rookie of the Year in 2003-2004. He played on the 2004 USA Olympic basketball team. He has been voted to play in the NBA All-Star Game twice in his first three NBA seasons (2005, 2006). And, he is the youngest player ever to reach 2,000 career points. This success all came before LeBron reached his 22nd birthday on December 30, 2006. Not a bad start to a career!

The sky is the limit for the young Cleveland Cavaliers' superstar.

While still in high school with the SVSM Irish, LeBron played in a game televised across the country by ESPN2.

CHAPTER 1

A Basketball Star Is Born

LEBRON JAMES WAS BORN ON DECEMBER 30, 1984. Two months earlier the great Michael Jordan had made his NBA rookie debut for the Chicago Bulls. By the time LeBron was in his teens, he was being compared to Jordan.

LeBron grew up in Akron, Ohio, a **blue-collar** factory town. He had a tough childhood. His mother, Gloria, was only 16 years old when she gave birth to him. LeBron never met his dad. He and Gloria drifted from one apartment to the next. Once, they were forced to move after their building was declared unsafe by the city of Akron and then bulldozed.

"I saw drugs, guns, killings; it was crazy," LeBron told *Sports Illustrated*. "But my mom kept food in my mouth and clothes on my back."

When LeBron was 10 years old, he moved in with the family of his youth basketball coach, Frankie Walker. LeBron said that living with Walker "changed my life." Frankie kept LeBron in line. In the 4th grade, LeBron had missed more than 100 days of school. In the 5th grade, when he lived with the Walkers, LeBron told S.I.,"I had perfect attendance and a B average."

As an 8th grader, LeBron led his local Akron team to the finals of a national AAU (**Amateur** Athletic Union) tournament. After 8th grade, LeBron enrolled at St. Vincent–St. Mary's, a small Catholic high school in Akron. As a freshman he averaged 18 points and 6 rebounds. SVSM finished 27–0 and won the Ohio Division III state championship.

SVSM won its second state title when LeBron was a sophomore. That year the whiz kid who wore number 23, just like Jordan, averaged 25 points, 7 rebounds, and nearly 6 assists per game. He won his first Ohio Mr. Basketball award as the state's best player. LeBron also played wide receiver for the football team and was named All-State in that sport.

In the summer between his sophomore and junior years of high school, LeBron became a high

Their lives were not always easy, but LeBron and his mom Gloria always found something to smile about.

school legend. At an Adidas ABCD Camp, a showcase for the top high school basketball players in the country, he dominated the best of the best. He averaged 29 points and nine rebounds per game and was named the camp's MVP.

The skills of the kid with the nickname "King James" were now well known. Michael Jordan invited him to play in his top-secret summer workouts in Chicago along with college and NBA players.

In LeBron's junior year, SVSM journeyed to Trenton, New Jersey, to play the No. 1 team in the nation, Oak Hill (Virginia) Academy. LeBron scored 36 points, but his Fighting Irish team lost, 72–66.

By that time, LeBron was the biggest sports celebrity in Akron, if not all of Ohio. SVSM moved its

Often playing before enormous crowds, LeBron amazed fans with his amazing dunks and high-flying play.

home games to a college arena and more than 4,000 fans attended each game. Nearly 1,800 fans bought season tickets, which is unheard of in high school basketball.

Still, even more fans wanted to see LeBron in action. After he won a second Mr. Basketball award as a junior (the team lost in the state semifinals), the entire country wanted to see him play. On December 12, 2002, ESPN2 televised a rematch between SVSM and Oak Hill. Dick Vitale and Bill Walton, both Basketball Hall of Fame inductees, called the game. It was the first high school basketball game ESPN had televised in 13 years.

LeBron's national television debut was a success. SVSM beat Oak Hill easily, 65–45. "King" James scored 31 points and had 13 rebounds as well as a few highlight dunks and no-look-pass assists.

"I'm leaving here more impressed than when I came in," said Walton, a former college and NBA star.

"He's amazing people at the age of 17," Michael Jordan said after that game. "From everything I've seen thus far, he's on the right track."

That he was. But King James' express train to the top was about to get derailed.

Most high school teams play in front of several hundred fans, usually students and families. LeBron's popularity broke new ground in high school hoops.

CHAPTER 2

First Trouble, Then Triumph

THE YEAR 2003 BEGAN WITH LEBRON JAMES living a life fit for royalty. On December 22nd in Philadelphia, 76ers star Allen Iverson watched LeBron, now a senior, and his team play local powerhouse Strawberry Mansion. Six days later, 18,000 fans jammed Ohio State University's basketball arena to watch the Fighting Irish stay unbeaten with an overtime win against Columbus (Ohio) Brookhaven. On December 30th, LeBron celebrated his 18th birthday with 30 friends at a Dave & Buster's, a video game palace and restaurant, in Cleveland.

LeBron James was officially the greatest basketball player in the world who still had to go to homeroom. In the first week of January, SVSM

LeBron leads his team onto the court in front of another packed arena. One of his skills is making his teammates play better.

traveled to Los Angeles. The Fighting Irish played in Pauley Pavilion, the famous home court of college power UCLA, and knocked off Santa Ana (California) Mater Dei, the No. 4 team in the nation. SVSM now had the No. 1-ranked boys team in the country.

After coming back from a controversial suspension, LeBron scored 52 points against a team from Los Angeles.

Friends and family started to shower LeBron with gifts to celebrate his success. But, some of those gifts caused trouble. High school athletes are not allowed to accept money or presents given to them because of their fame. Receiving gifts or money violates their amateur athletic status. Pro athletes get paid. Amateur athletes, like high school and college players, do not.

LeBron's mother, Gloria, gave him a Hummer H2 for his birthday. The expensive vehicle made people **suspicious**. How did Gloria afford such a fancy car? People suspected she had been given money by a sports agent to buy the car. She soon proved she took out a loan from a bank to get the money.

Then, on January 31, LeBron was **suspended** for two games by the Ohio High School Athletic Association. He had accepted two sports jerseys from a local sports store worth $845.

In his first game back after his suspension, LeBron scored a career-high 52 points against the No. 7 team in the nation, Westchester of Los Angeles. LeBron's individual points matched Westchester's team total in the 78–52 win.

"This court, this basketball court, is like my house," LeBron said. "I think missing [games] gave me a little more **motivation**."

St. Vincent–St. Mary's did not lose again that season. LeBron averaged 31 points and nearly 10 rebounds as SVSM finished 25–1. The Fighting Irish

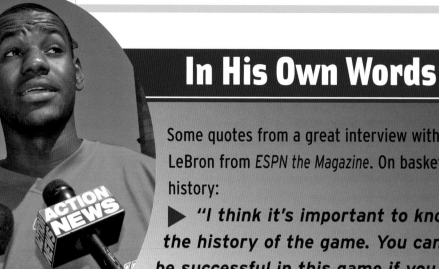

In His Own Words

Some quotes from a great interview with LeBron from *ESPN the Magazine*. On basketball history:

▶ *"I think it's important to know the history of the game. You can't be successful in this game if you don't know who got you to this point. Unfortunately, a lot of people my age and younger don't know the history of basketball."*

On whom he patterns his game after:

▶ *"I don't try to pattern my game after anybody's, but if I had to talk about similarities, I'd look at Penny Hardaway when he was in Orlando. He was a 6'7" point guard. He had flair, he could pass, he'd dunk on you and he could shoot jumpers."*

On being compared to NBA legends Oscar Robertson and Magic Johnson:

▶ *"I don't say I'm going to try to be those guys, but I can see a little bit of my game in each of them. And I'm not really concerned about surpassing them in history. I just hope that one day people will think I was one of the best players to ever play in this league. Ever. I know that'll take titles, though."*

won their third Division III state championship in LeBron's fourth season at the school. LeBron also won his third Ohio Mr. Basketball award in a row. SVSM was voted national champions by *USA Today*. LeBron finished his high school career with 2,657 points and 892 rebounds. St. Vincent-St. Mary's retired his No. 23 jersey.

With LeBron's high school career completed, the only question left was whether he would accept a college scholarship or go directly to the NBA. First, LeBron wanted to play in high school All-Star games featuring the nation's top seniors. In the McDonald's All-America game in Cleveland, LeBron scored 27 points and was named MVP as he led his East team to victory.

A few days later in Chicago, LeBron added to his legend at the Roundball Classic. With his East team losing by one point with 24 seconds left, King James grabbed a

LeBron and sprinter Allyson Felix were the national high school athletes of the year in 2003.

LeBron was the best of the best at the McDonald's All-America all-star game. The games showcased his talents for the NBA.

rebound and dribbled the length of the court. He hit the game-winning lay-up in front of more than 19,000 fans. He finished the evening with 28 points and earned his second All-Star game MVP award in one week.

There was one more All-Star game left to play, the Capital Classic in Washington, D.C. However, if a high school senior plays in more than two All-Star games, he must sit out his first year of college basketball. LeBron made it clear he was going straight to the NBA by playing in the All-Star game. More than 18,000 fans and 300 journalists attended the game. LeBron's idol, Michael Jordan, was also in the crowd.

LeBron put on a spectacular show for all of them. He scored 34 points and had 12 rebounds, but his team lost.

"If it would have been my last game at the high school level, ending with a loss, I'd be upset," LeBron said after the game. "But tonight I was just here to have fun. I loved every minute of it."

Two months later, LeBron's biggest dream came true. On June 26, 2003, NBA commissioner David Stern stepped up to a podium at the NBA draft and announced: "With the first pick of the 2003 NBA draft, the Cleveland Cavaliers select LeBron James."

A new era in the NBA had begun.

Colleges looking to add to their teams watch high school all-star games. As more players go right from high school to the NBA, pro scouts are paying close attention, too.

There was no doubt that the Cavaliers would make their new number 23 their number one pick in 2003.

CHAPTER 3

King James and His New Court

MORE THAN 15,000 FANS PACKED A GYM IN Orlando, Florida, in July of 2003 for a summer league game between the Orlando Magic and the Cleveland Cavaliers. Normally, a summer league game would have drawn just hundreds of spectators. But this game was different. LeBron was playing for the Cavs.

Before King James even scored his first pro bucket, he was elbowed to the floor by Orlando Magic forward Alton Ford. The elbow was his "Welcome to the NBA" moment. Less than a minute later, LeBron stole an **outlet pass** from Ford and dunked the ball. He had scored his first basket against NBA players. Although he played just less than half the game, LeBron scored 14 points.

"I don't know why you keep calling him a kid,"

Magic guard Keith Bogans, who guarded LeBron, told the media later. "He's a man now."

LeBron made his regular-season NBA debut on October 29, 2003, against the Sacramento Kings. Playing point guard, King James scored 25 points and had nine assists and six rebounds. No player who

LeBron's rookie season had its share of ups and downs, but mostly ups.

had gone straight from high school to the NBA had ever scored that many points in his first game.

Before the season, LeBron had signed a $90 million endorsement deal with Nike. It was the richest such deal for an athlete in sports history. Even super golfer Tiger Woods does not take that much from one sponsor.

The deal with Nike was well earned. In LeBron's rookie season he averaged 20.9 points, 5.5 rebounds and 5.9 assists. Only Michael Jordan and Oscar Robertson, two of the NBA's all-time greats, had also averaged 20 points and more than 5 assists and rebounds per game in their rookie years. LeBron was voted NBA Rookie of the Year.

LeBron's rookie stats were similar to those of the great Oscar Robertson.

LeBron also made the Cavaliers a much-improved team. In the season before he arrived, Cleveland won just 17 games. With LeBron in a Cavalier uniform, the franchise more than doubled its win total, finishing with a final regular-season record of 35–47.

The Cavs did not make the playoffs, but LeBron still did not have much time off between his rookie year and second NBA season. In the summer of 2004, he played for the U.S. men's basketball team at the Summer Olympics. The team won the bronze medal.

After sporting the "USA" basketball jersey, LeBron wore his first NBA All-Star jersey during the 2004-2005 season. He was voted as starter for the East squad. LeBron helped the East snap a three-game losing streak to the West in a 125–115 victory. LeBron scored 13 points and added 8 rebounds and 6 assists.

LeBron also helped the Cavaliers improve in their second season together. In November, the Cavs trailed by 19 points in the fourth quarter to the Phoenix Suns. The Suns were one of the NBA's top teams. LeBron scored 38 points and grabbed 10 rebounds and Cleveland won the game, 114–109, in overtime.

Although the team failed to make the playoffs again, LeBron still led his team to a winning record (42–40). Near the end of the season, he also had some

Prior to 1992, the U.S. Olympic basketball team was made of all college players. After that point, NBA players have been chosen to play for the U.S.

Though he was still a teenager, LeBron joined the NBA's best in helping the U.S. win a bronze medal at the 2004 Olympics.

His Big Moment

Simply putting on an NBA uniform was a dream come true for LeBron James. It was something he had wished for since he was big enough to bounce a basketball. To have that dream come true in such a marvelously big way made it one for the ages.

LeBron's first regular-season NBA game came along with enormous expectations of the 18-year-old star. Hundreds of reporters from literally around the world (Taiwan and Japan sent reporters) descended on Sacramento, where LeBron's Cavaliers were to play the hometown Kings. LeBron's mom was in attendance along with stars from other sports and dozens of celebrities. It was the "must-see" sports event of the season. If LeBron had gone out and clanked, it might have made his life as a pro very difficult. On an evening when it would have been understood if the teenager were distracted, he excelled. He had his first assist in the second minute, his first score a few moments later. He was on his way.

of the best games of his young NBA career. On March 20, he scored a career-high 56 points in a 105–98 road loss to the Toronto Raptors. LeBron, who was 20 at the time, became the youngest player in NBA history to score 50 points in one game. But the point total didn't mean much to him.

NBA All-Star Games are always a big, glamorous show, and LeBron has made shining in them a specialty.

LeBron's sterling career won't be complete without an NBA title.

"I played well, probably the best game of my life, but it means nothing when you come away with a loss," said LeBron. "I don't care about individual stats, especially when you lose."

LeBron finished the season averaging 27.2 points and more than 7 rebounds and 7 assists per game. Only four players in the history of the NBA ever averaged 25, 7 and 7 in one season. All four are in now the Hall of Fame.

LeBron James has accomplished more on a basketball court at his age than anyone else before him. But for now he wants to focus on one thing: Winning a championship.

I want to stay with the Cavs and build a champion," he told *ESPN The Magazine*. "I feel like we're on our way."

LeBron James's
Career Statistics

Year	Team	G	FG%	RPG	APG	PPG
2003-04	CLE	79	.417	5.5	5.9	20.9
2004-05	CLE	80	.472	7.4	7.2	27.2
2005-06	CLE	68	.473	7.2	6.7	30.8
Career		227	.455	6.7	6.6	26.1

Legend: **CLE**: Cleveland; **G**: games; **FG%**: field goal percentage; **RPG**: average rebounds per game; **APG**: average assists per game; **PPG**: average points scored per game

GLOSSARY

amateur a person who is not paid to perform a certain skill, in this case basketball

blue-collar referring to people who work with their hands, compared to white-collar workers who work in offices

hype exaggerated promotion of an event or person

motivation inspiration or desire to succeed or perform a task

outlet pass a basketball pass made to a teammate running down the court toward his team's basket

suspended temporarily prevented from taking part in something due to a rules violation

suspicious having a feeling that something is wrong

BOOKS

King James: Believe the Hype, The LeBron James Story
By Ryan Jones
(St. Martin's, New York) 2003
This book is a full biography of James's life prior to his turning professional and entering the NBA.

LeBron James
By John Hareas
(Scholastic, New York) 2005
This official NBA book addresses the hype James faced upon entering the NBA draft and focuses on the pressure surrounding his rookie season.

LeBron James
By Mark Stewart
(Raintree, Chicago) 2005
This biography features color action photographs and includes fact boxes and interviews.

LeBron James: King On and Off the Court
By Ken Rappoport
(Enslow Publishers, New Jersey) 2006
This book covers James's basketball life while also focusing on his family life and childhood influences.

LeBron James: The Rise of a Star
By David Lee Morgan Jr.
(Gray & Company Publishers, Cleveland) 2003
This book draws its material from interviews with family, friends, coaches and teammates. It also includes lots of color photographs of James from toddler to pro athlete.

WEB SITES

Visit our home page for lots of links about LeBron James:
www.childsworld.com/links

Note to Parents, Teachers, and Librarians: We routinely check our Web links to make sure they're safe, active sites—so encourage your readers to check them out!

ABOUT THE AUTHOR

John Walters, a former staff writer for *Sports Illustrated*, is the author of several basketball books, including *Basketball for Dummies* (cowritten with former Notre Dame coach Digger Phelps) and *Same River Twice*, about the University of Connecticut women's team.